GREEN *Poetry*

Selected by
Robert Hull

Illustrated by
Annabel Spenceley

Thematic Poetry

Also available:

Animal Poetry
Christmas Poetry
Day and Night Poetry
Food Poetry

Houses and Homes Poetry
Science Poetry
Sea Poetry

Series editor: Catherine Ellis
Designer: Derek Lee

First published in 1991 by
Wayland (Publishers) Ltd
61 Western Road, Hove
East Sussex BN3 1JD, England

© Copyright 1991 Wayland
(Publishers) Ltd

**British Library Cataloguing in
Publication Data**
Green poetry. – (Thematic Poetry)
  I. Hull, Robert   II. Spenceley,
  Annabel   III. Series
  821.9140809282

HARDBACK ISBN 0-7502-0082-0

PAPERBACK ISBN 0-7502-0935-6

Picture Acknowledgements
The publishers would like to thank the
following for allowing their illustrations to
be reproduced in this book: Ardea 15;
Bruce Coleman Ltd. 5 (Gerald Cubitt), 10
(Jen & Des Bartlett), 22 (Geoff Dore), 37
(Frank Greenaway) 41 (Jeff Foott); The
Environmental Picture Library 9 (P
Glendell); Eye Ubiquitous 21, 35 (Helen A.
Lisher); Frank Lane Picture Agency 30
(Michael Clark); Oxford Scientific Films
back cover, 19 (Kjell B Sandved), 29 (Stan
Osolinski), 38 (Partridge Productions Ltd.),
44 (St Meyers); Topham 13; Zefa *front
cover*, 7, 16 (Rheinhard), 24 (Mueller), 32,
43 (E & P Bauer).

Acknowledgements
For permission to reprint copyright
material the publishers gratefully
acknowledge the following: Cadbury Ltd
for Kathryn Boydell's 'A mouse lived in a
laboratory', and Edward Turnbull's 'Who
killed the swan?'; excerpts from *An
Introduction to Haiku* by Harold G.
Henderson, copyright © 1958 Harold G.
Henderson, used by permission of
Doubleday, a division of Bantam
Doubleday Dell Publishing Group Inc.;
'Take one home for the kiddies' reprinted
by permission of Faber and Faber Ltd from
Whitsun Weddings by Philip Larkin; 'In my
garden' by Charles Causley reprinted by
permission of David Higham Associates
from *Early in the morning*; Katie Campbell
for 'Belugas'; Paul Coltman for 'Toad';
Kevin McCann for 'In the museum of past
centuries'; Brian Moses for 'Problems';
Irene Rawnsley for 'This Elephant';
Duncan Thomas for 'The day they had to
get proper artesian well-water for the pigs
at the show', and 'Poet talking about his
poem written on recycled paper helping
. . . '; Raymond Wilson for 'This letter's to
say'; 'Four Little Tigers' by Frank Jacobs
reprinted by permission of Mad Magazine
and (© 1972 by E.C. Publications Inc.).
While every effort has been made to trace
the copyright holders, in some cases it has
proved impossible. The publishers
apologise for this apparent negligence.

Typeset by Rachel Gibbs, Wayland
Printed in Italy by G. Canale & C.S.p.A.,
Turin

Contents

Introduction

Green poems? What on earth are they? Poems aren't green, they're black, black marks on white pages. The next thing you know, teachers will start talking about blue history . . . or purple sums . . . or pink . . .

Well, perhaps they will perhaps they won't, but many people certainly have started 'talking green', wondering about ways to keep on having elephants for jungles, and jungles for elephants. They want to keep our earth brimming and healthy, and pollute it less. They want to give more of a greeting to its life, by saying things like 'Welcome whales' instead of harpooning them and batting their heads in.

When the Indian Chief Seattle says, 'the horse and the eagle are our brothers, flowers and plants our sisters', he is greeting all kinds of life, celebrating them. And when an Ojibway Indian says, 'The bush is sitting under a tree and singing', what he's doing is seeing a small bush look happy. His words may sound strange, but we say bushes and trees 'look sad' during a drought, so it should make sense to say a bush or a tree or bit of jungle looks happy, happy enough to sing. If you were a bit of jungle and somebody decided not to chop you down you might feel like a chorus or two yourself.

Everyone feels 'green' like this sometimes, in different ways, about all the kinds of life on earth. Like the life of the wet and the weeds and the wilderness that Gerard Manley Hopkins celebrated a hundred years ago, though he was a bit anxious about them even then:

'What would the world be, once bereft
Of wet and wilderness? Let them be left,
O let them be left, wildness and wet;
Long live the weeds and the wilderness yet.'

Have you ever thought, 'O let them be left'? What about? When do you have your green moments and moods? Or your green 'Problems', like the girl in Brian Moses' poem? Tell us in poems.

How can one sell the air?

We shall consider your offer
to buy our land.
What is it that the White Man wants to buy?
my people will ask.

How can one sell the air
or buy the warmth of the earth?
It is difficult for us to imagine.
If we don't own the sweet air
or the bubbling water,
how can you buy it from us?
Each hillside of pines shining in the sun,
each sandy beach and rocky river bank,
every steep valley with bees humming
or mists hanging in dark woods,
has been made sacred by some event
in the memory of our people.

We are part of the earth
and the earth is part of us.
The fragrant flowers are our sisters;
the reindeer, the horse,
the great eagles, are our brothers.
The foamy crests of waves in the river,
the sap of meadow flowers,
the pony's sweat and the man's sweat
are one and the same thing.
So when the Great Chief in Washington
sends word that he wants to buy all these things,
we find it hard to understand.

CHIEF SEATTLE

Problems

A voice was saying on Breakfast TV
how we should be taking more care
of our planet; and I thought between bites
of toast and jam, it really must
get untidy sometimes. I wondered
if God ever shouted out loud,
like mum when my room's in a dreadful state:
Hey, you lot, isn't it time
you set to work and tidied your planet?
Then another voice said, this world
is sick, and I wondered how he knew.
You could hardly feel its nose
like a dog, or shove a thermometer
under its tongue. Such problems were
far too complicated and I needed
expert advice, but my teacher
didn't know when I asked and joked that
she only knew where to look when
answers came out of a book. She told me,
instead, that my maths was a mess
and my handwriting wasn't tidy.
She didn't seem to understand,
I had bigger problems weighting my mind.

BRIAN MOSES

This Elephant

lives on a reel of film
in a tin container.

This elephant
eats leaves
and green bananas through
an hour of documentary.

This elephant
likes mud,
enjoys a squirt at waterholes
with her companions.

This elephant
loves her calf,
charges cross-tusked
at cameras come to shoot it.

This elephant
walked miles
on ancestral elephant tracks
to appear on tonight's TV

This elephant
died for ivory yesterday.

IRENE RAWNSLEY

A Mouse Lived in a Laboratory

The scientists dyed a mouse bright blue
To see what all its friends would do.
Its friends, they didn't seem to mind . . .
The scientists wrote down their find.

The scientists cut the mouse's brain
To see if it would act the same.
The mouse was still able to think . . .
The scientists wrote this down, in ink.

The scientists took the mouse's brain
Clumsily sewed it up again.
The mouse, it acted like a clown . . .
The scientists wrote all this down.

The scientists tied the mouse's feet
And buried it in soil and peat
The mouse quite liked it in the muck . . .
The scientists wrote this in their book.

Soon afterwards the scientists tried
To spin the mouse until it died.
The mouse loved whirring round and round . . .
(The scientists' pad was spiral bound.)

The mouse, by now immune to pain,
Could not have been of use again.
Red cross through notes, and 'Mouse no good'.
The scientists wrote this down.
In blood.

KATHRYN BOYDELL (Aged 15)

13

Three Haiku

Little frog
  don't give up the fight!
    Issa is here!

        Oh don't mis-treat
            the fly! he wrings his hands!
              He wrings his feet!

Little sparrow, take care!
  Get out of the way! – Mr Horse
    is coming there!

ISSA

Toad

There was a toad lived in a drain,
sheltered from frost and wind and rain;
while overhead we bathed our daughters
and sprinkled him with tepid waters.

So damp and dark and safe from view
toad like a fungus sat and grew.
Cold as wet stone, on stone he lay,
and took whatever came his way.
He shared our water, made no fuss,
in a small way seemed one of us.

But life is never free from troubles;
the girls began to bath in bubbles.
Poor toad, bewildered by the spray,
emerged and stiffly walked away.

We have not seen him since that day.

PAUL COLTMAN

The day they had to get proper artesian well-water for the pigs at the show

The pigs wouldn't drink
the water (London
tap).

'It might be unwise to drink'
(I heard one sniff)
'that!'

They must have picked
up the faintest
whiff

of something
a bit iff-
y off

the water all us
Londoners
drink,

a not-nice (for pigs)
trace of a
stink

of something they know
won't keep pigs
in the pink.

So, at the show,
they turn up delicate
snouts at it:

'For porcine consumption
this water's quite un-
fit,

bring us proper
artesian water.
Jump to it.'

DUNCAN THOMAS

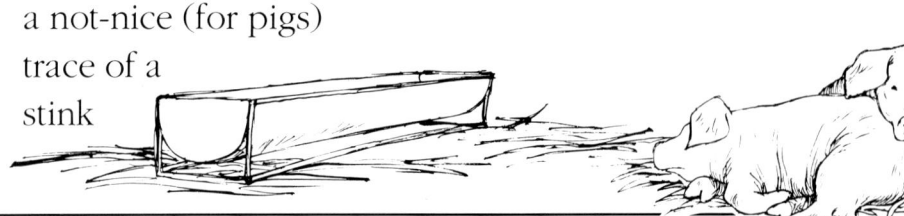

Take One Home for the Kiddies

On shallow straw, in shadeless glass,
Huddled by empty bowls, they sleep:
No dark, no dam, no earth, no grass –
Mam, get us one of them to keep.

Living toys are something novel,
But it soon wears off somehow.
Fetch the shoebox, fetch the shovel –
Mam, we're playing funerals now.

PHILIP LARKIN

In My Garden

In my garden
Grows a tree
Dances day
And night for me,
Four in a bar
Or sometimes three
To music secret
As can be.

Nightly to
Its hidden tune
I watch it move
Against the moon,
Dancing to
A silent sound,
One foot planted
In the ground.

Dancing tree,
When may I hear
Day or night
Your music clear?
What the note
And what the song
That you sing
The seasons long?

It is written,
Said the tree,
On the pages
Of the sea;
It is there
At every hand
On the pages
Of the land;

Whether waking
Or in dream:
Voice of meadow-grass
And stream,
And out of
The ringing air
Voice of sun
And moon and star.

It is there
For all to know
As tides shall turn
And wildflowers grow;
There for you
And there for me,
Said the glancing
Dancing tree.

CHARLES CAUSLEY

The Poplar Field

The poplars are fell'd, farewell to the shade
And the whispering sound of the cool colonnade;
The winds play no longer and sing in the leaves,
Nor Ouse on his bosom their image receives.

Twelve years have elapsed since I last took a view
Of my favourite field, and the bank where they grew.
And now in the grass behold they are laid,
And the tree is my seat that once lent me a shade.

WILLIAM COWPER

Poet talking about his poem written on recycled paper helping . . .

I'm writing this on re-
cycled paper, 'Helping to use
the earth's resources economically',
it says

in nice brown ink under a green
tree on the back
of the exercise-book
I write poems in.

I suppose it's alright to write
if we don't use
too much paper and chop down
too many of you, trees,

so I've started to write poems
with the fewest words I can in
though even in this one
perhaps I could have written less (sorry,

fewer) words and crossed out some.
But, in future, trees,
I'll be writing economicaller
stories and poems (see? 'Economicaller'

's shorter than 'more economical' – *and*
comicaller) and if they keep on dwindling
like rain forests and ice-fields
I'll soon be an earth-preserving

sort of writer writing hardly anything,
which could be a good thing
– for the environment I mean.
(I'd written all this down

last night then suddenly
in my dream this falling
tree
yells, 'Who are you kidding,

Just who
do
you
think you're kidding?')

DUNCAN THOMAS

A Message to the Moon

You're not as dead as you look.
They're after you.
They'll strike oil on you.
They'll build refineries on your forehead
and run freeways from your eyes to your mouth.
They'll fill your pores with scrap iron
and your nostrils with smog.
Your chin will break out in a rash of billboards
and your cheeks will be pockmarked with trailer camps.
Try to look deader. Forget to wax.
Keep on waning. Get off your orbit.
Eclipse!
Don't just sit there mooning.

MILLICENT L. PETTIT

This Letter's to Say

Dear Sir or Madam,
This letter's to say
Your property
Stands bang in the way
Of Progress, and
Will be knocked down
On March the third
At half-past one.

There is no appeal,
Since the National Need
Depends on more
And still more Speed,
And this, in turn,
Dear Sir or Madam,
Depends on half England
Being tar-macadam.
(But your house will –
We are pleased to say –
Be the fastest lane
Of the Motorway).

Meanwhile the Borough
Corporation
Offer you new
Accommodation
Three miles away
On the thirteenth floor
(Flat Number Q 6824).

But please take note,
The Council regret:
No dog, cat, bird

Or other pet;
No noise permitted,
No singing in the bath
(For permits to drink
Or smoke or laugh
Apply on Form Z327);
No children admitted
Aged under eleven;
No hawkers, tramps
Or roof-top lunchers;
No opening doors
To Bible-punchers.

Failure to pay
Your rent, when due,
Will lead to our
Evicting you.
The Council demand
That you consent
To the terms above
When you pay your rent.

Meanwhile we hope
You will feel free
To consult us
Should there prove to be
The slightest case
Of difficulty.

With kind regards;
Yours faithfully . . .

RAYMOND WILSON

31

Big Yellow Taxi

They paved paradise
And put up a parking lot
With a pink hotel, a boutique
And a swinging hot spot
Don't it always seem to go
That you don't know what you've got
Till it's gone
They paved paradise
And put up a parking lot.

They took all the trees
And put them in a tree museum
And they charged all the people
A dollar and a half just to see 'em
Don't it always seem to go
That you don't know what you've got
Till it's gone
They paved paradise
And put up a parking lot.

Hey farmer farmer
Put away that DDT now
Give me spots on my apples
But leave me the birds and the bees
Please!
Don't it always seem to go
That you don't know what you've got
Till it's gone
They paved paradise
And put up a parking lot.

Late last night
I heard the screen door slam
And a big yellow taxi
Took away my old man
Don't it always seem to go
That you don't know what you've got
Till it's gone
They paved paradise
And put up a parking lot.

JONI MITCHELL

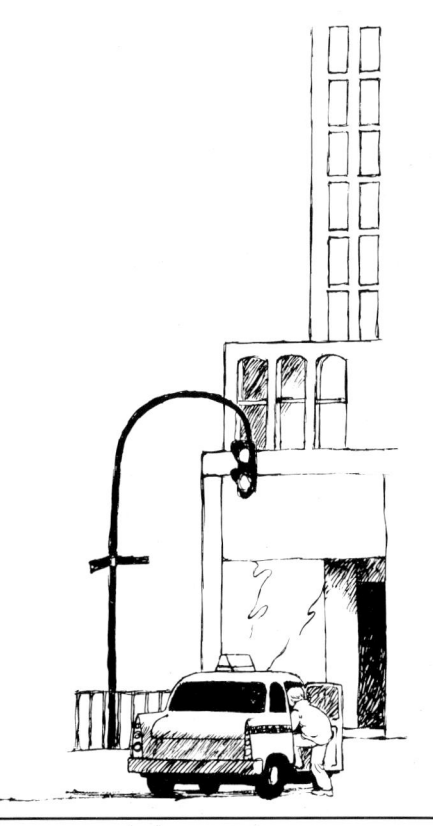

Who Killed the Swan?

Who killed the swan?
'I,' said the weight,
'My poison lead she ate,
I killed the swan.'

Who left it there?
'I,' said the fisherman,
'When my day was done.
I left it there.'

Who saw her die?
'We,' said the reeds,
'She fell amongst our leaves.
We saw her die.'

Who will mourn her passing?
'I,' said the water,
'For she was my daughter.
I will mourn her passing.'

EDWARD TURNBULL (Aged 14)

In the Museum of Past Centuries

We have

Elephant tusks, a grey seal,
The songs of a Blue Whale,
White snow, green fields,
The Rain Forest's very last tree.

In the Museum
Of Past Centuries
We have

English wolves,
Dodo birds,
Aztecs, Incas,
Tasmanian Aborigines.

In the Museum
Of Past Centuries
We have

Stinking rivers,
Acid lakes,
Dying fish,
Dead seas.

In the Museum
Of Past Centuries
We have

Mustard gas,
Barbed wire,
Atom bombs,
A lead container
Marked 'Deadly'.

In the Museum
Of Past Centuries
We have

(Standing alone)
A single glass case,
Inside, an apple
That's been bitten twice:
Old, tempting and juicy.

KEVIN McCANN

The Brontosaurus

The Brontosaurus
Had a brain
No bigger than
A crisp;

The Dodo
Had a stammer
And the Mammoth
Had a lisp;

The Auk
Was just too Aukward –
Now they're none of them
Alive.

Each one,
(Like Man)
Had shown himself
Unfitted to survive.

This story
Points a moral:
Now it's
We
Who wear the pants:

The extinction
Of these species
Holds a lesson
For us
ANTS.

MICHAEL FLANDERS

Belugas

In the flickering glare of the late news
before switching off for the night –
suddenly caught by familiar white
Belugas

those vast arctic angels
sailing south, seeking plankton
which thrives where the salt St. Lawrence
swirls at a place called

'Tadoussac'
mispronounced by the British reporter
shoring himself ineffectively
from the withering wind off the water.

Raw-fingered, gripping his mike too close
he discloses:

factory waste spewed by the ton, by the minute,
washing up corpses on sandcastle shores
not whales now, not mammals, they're toxic waste sites now.
– And disposed of accordingly.

But here, on TV, they still swim, grinning greenly
cavorting in close-up, a three minute item
lodged between hard news and sports
on a slow day –

those innocent angels
returned to my life in this late night
an ocean, a childhood away
claiming their brief span of fame.

KATIE CAMPBELL

Four Little Tigers

Four little tigers
Sitting in a tree;
One became a lady's coat –
And now there are three.

Three little tigers
'Neath a sky of blue;
One became a rich man's rug –
Now there's only two.

Two little tigers
Sitting in the sun;
One a hunter's trophy made –
Now there's only one.

One little tiger
Waiting to be had;
Oops! he got the hunter first –
Aren't you kind of glad?

FRANK JACOBS

Minstrel's Song

There are, some people say, no riches in the bush.
But look at an ant hill:
It has a helmet providing shelter from the rain.
See that beetle:
His coat does not go round him
And yet it has three buttons.
A bird which lives there in the bush
Has a wooden house:
Who is the carpenter?
This bush cow wears boots
Like those of a soldier;
That baboon has a black coat
Like a policeman;
And the kingfisher has a silk gown.
Why, then, do some people say
There are no riches in the bush?

ANON. (Translated from Mende by K. L. Little)

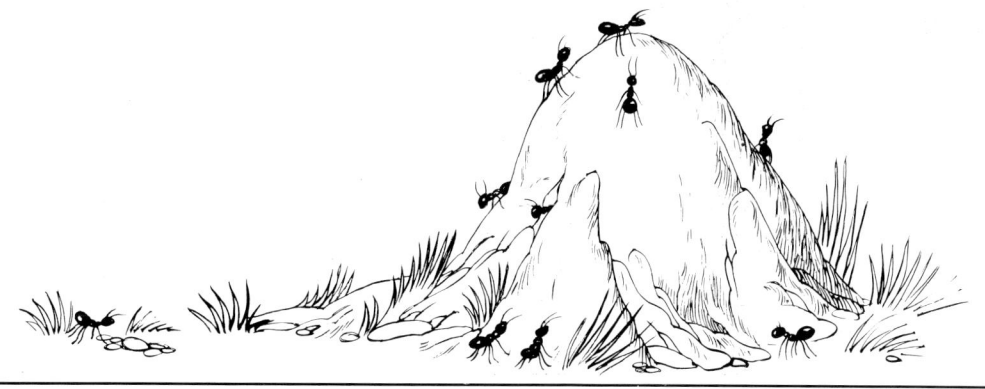

Biographies

Katie Campbell is a Canadian writer who lives in London. She contributes regularly to the *Guardian*, and writes plays, short stories and poems. Her collection of short stories is called *What He Really Wants Is A Dog*.

Charles Causley was born in Cornwall, where he still lives. He was in the Royal Navy, then was a schoolteacher for twenty-five years. He is one of the most famous writers of poems for children.

Paul Coltman lives in Sussex. He has two collections of poems for adults, and two books for children, the very well-known *Tog the Ribber* – with illustrations by his daughter, Gillian McClure – and *Witch Watch*. A third children's book, *Tinker Jim*, is coming out soon.

William Cowper lived in England from 1731 to 1800. His name is pronounced 'Cooper'. He wrote hymns as well as poetry.

Michael Flanders was born in 1922. He went to Oxford University and was on the way to becoming an outstanding actor when he caught polio in 1943. He fought his way back to health and made a career as a famous writer of witty song-lyrics. He also invented one or two ingenious gardening tools for the disabled.

In Japan, **Issa** (1762–1826) is the most popular of all haiku writers. He had a sad life. His last poem was found under his pillow in the cold room without windows that he'd moved into after his house burned down. Stories say that he went about badly dressed, and was sometimes rude to important people.

Philip Larkin (1922–85) was one of the most famous British poets of this century. He didn't write specially for children, but a few of his poems do appeal to them.

Kevin McCann was born in Widnes but grew up in Blackpool. He has written poems for as long as he can remember and published two books for adults. He worked for twelve years as a teacher, but is now a professional writer. At present he is writing a book of poems for children.

Joni Mitchell was a pop singer in the 1960s. The poem we have included is the lyrics from one of her songs.

Brian Moses was a teacher, and is now a freelance writer living in Sussex. He visits schools doing writing workshops and performances. Many of his poems for children have been published in anthologies, and his collection *Leave Your Teddy Behind* was published in 1988.

Irene Rawnsley lives in Settle, Yorkshire. In 1988 Methuen published a collection of her poems for children called *Ask a Silly Question*, and a second book, called *Dog's Dinner*, is due out in 1990.

Chief Seattle's real name was Sealth. He was a chief among the Duwamish Indians of North West America. The extract we have chosen is actually from a speech he made in 1854 to the Governor of Washington Territory, while they were arranging a treaty. The speech was copied down by Dr Henry Smith, a neighbour of Sealth who knew the Duwamish language.

Edward Turnbull was at St David's Secondary School in Acklam, Middlesborough, aged 14, when his poem was written. We guess he'll be 18 now, but don't know anything more about him.

Raymond Wilson is a well-known collector and editor of poems for children, and a poet himself. He is also Professor of Education at Reading University.

Index of first lines